Publication Assistance and Printing Services by IngramSpark
www.ingramspark.com

Published by Darrell Keezer

ISBN 978-0-9939457-0-0
E-Book: ISBN 978-0-9939457-1-7

First Edition: October 2014

Printed in the United States of America

Text set in Adobe Garmond Pro
Cover and header text set in Mr Eaves Modern OT by Emigre Fonts,
Emigre Fonts retains ownership of the trademarks and copyrights
www.fontshop.com

Edited by Leigh Colgan
Illustrations and design by Rebecca De Girolamo,
rebecca.degirolamo@gmail.com

Your Website Died 37 Times

INTRODUCTION

Do you remember the excitement you felt launching your company's first website and the thrill of proclaiming from the virtual rooftops that your company existed? Do you recall the effort exerted to get a few static pages to go live or how your staff had to change their email footers to include the brand new *online presence*? Remember the anticipation of new leads and ever increasing online sales?

And then the unimaginable disappointment; nothing changed and nothing happened. You struggled to keep the site updated. Every few years you would revisit this online mess of words, images, broken links and generic forms and wonder why it never produced a single piece of business, a lead or even one online sale. After all, that was the plan, wasn't it?

Now your website isn't just struggling to keep up, it is actually dead.

Not dead as in a "*404 – page not found*". It is still there, but it is dead in regards to communicating anything valuable to your end-customer or potential next big deal. It is dead to current trends, dead in front of prospects, dead to changing technologies, dead to where your company is headed, dead to your latest project. It cannot talk, listen, interact, sell or convince anyone that they should work with you.

What has made your experience worse is that every so often, a new web-design company has come along, pointed out how outdated your website is, and convinced you to build a new corpse to hang on your WWW for the next five years. It's depressing.

I've been there and I believe most businesses have been there. *"Our website doesn't generate us any business"*, is one of the most common statements I hear from business owners and marketing managers.

I believe that every website is a work in progress and "done" is never done, but a web-presence should at least be **alive**. It should be living and active, converting prospects into customers, and customers into advocates. It should be connecting people, resolving problems, and even generating revenue.

When I started Candybox Marketing in 2008, our sole purpose was to make the web sweet. Websites should engage and assist users, and leave them feeling satisfied with their experience.

We believe that every website can live, and become a strong web-presence. A presence lives online and encourages conversation and interaction, but a mere site is something that once was and is now long forgotten.

In the following chapters, I will highlight 37 different reasons why your website may have died, and what you can do about it. My suggestions may challenge the core of your marketing department, and shake up your task list each month, but the rewards will be sweet.

Imagine a web-presence that attracts, engages and converts prospects into customers, night and day. Where customers come to give you praise and contribute content for other users. Where you consider every improvement to your site, an investment, rather than an expense.

Why 37 times?

The internet is full of useless content and I am committed to not producing more of it. Why have we highlighted 37 website "deaths" and not 40 or 50? It's simple. I compiled a list of high-priority pitfalls that we most often encounter when working with clients. It just happened to be a list of 37. If I made it 40, I would have to make up 3 more just to fill space, and your time is worth much more than that.

You have nothing left to lose and a vibrant web-presence to gain, so let's do this. Enjoy the read.

- Darrell Keezer
Founder of Candybox Marketing

#1

Your Site is Objective-less

A visitor hits your site and then what? You have their attention for mere milliseconds. In a moment, images flash in front of their eyes and they make judgments, decisions and form a perception about your company that didn't exist seconds before. They judge your graphics, text, and calls to action faster than you can say 'bounce rate'. They scan your navigation, or lack thereof and think of where to go from there. They don't read a single sentence on your homepage because it is boring & irrelevant to them.

One of two things happen next: they go forward into your site, or they click the back button, exit the tab and continue on with life. This is the moment of truth that your entire web presence depends on, and in that moment visitors are looking for your direction on where to go next.

Most visitors are impatient, needy and used to attractive sites that are stupid-proof. They are demanding, judgmental and want answers in seconds.

In my experience, most businesses fail to think about this when they write their website content, choose their graphics and evaluate **what content to use on their homepage or landing pages.** If your users don't know what to do or where to go next, it is because **you have not thought through what you want them to do.**

Your website has failed to guide your users because you have not solidified your website objectives.

Solution:

Consider the main objectives that you want users to focus on for **every page of your website.**

Do you want them to get a quote? Give them a big 'Get a Quote' button. Do you want them to buy something? Make the checkout process simple and beautiful. Do you want them to submit their personal information? Consider why they would want to do that and give them an incentive to do so.

We recommend writing down 1-4 objectives for **every page** on your website and let your copywriting and designs follow this as a guide.

#2

Your Content is Dead

Website content is typically written by the wrong people. Simple web-design companies will usually impress you with their designs, and then request that you send them the content. This is an immediate death sentence for most website projects.

But there you go, sitting down to write out your content with a big cup of coffee at your desk, a blank document open with curser blinking, waiting for the inspiration to write out what you do.

If you're like most people, you probably start drafting your website content like an essay, beginning with a title, headings and then paragraph upon boring paragraph of body content. The content is about you, your company, your vision and maybe competitive advantages. Your final website draft looks more like content for a printed brochure than something that a user would want to read online. You forget that the buttons on your website are more important than the sentences that surround them, and you spend countless hours writing copy that will never be read, not even by the web-design company.

The big day comes when you get the first draft of your design and there is a big problem; it is **exactly** what you asked for. The design company has followed your directions

to the T, and you are now the proud owner of nothing more than an online brochure which you expect people to read.

Even if you hire a copywriter, they may do the same thing, but with better words. They think nothing of the user flow, dynamic information, buttons, navigation and calls to action. They are likely to produce a long document that looks good on paper, but is terrible online. Your website is now an outdated brochure that no one will read.

Solution:

Stop. Do not write the content. Hire a company that does content production / user experience for the web. Leave it up to online marketing experts to choose which words to put where. Let them produce wireframes before you start the design process. Let them present a user-flow and make sure it lines up with the objectives for each page. (See #1 website death). Don't do it yourself. Trust me.

Search Engines Think You're Dead.

If you produce a beautiful website that no one can ever find, does it even exist? If your website converts 50% of users into customers, but you only have a few hits per day, is it successful?

I have seen a lot of major outbound marketing campaigns on Radio, TV and Newspapers, push traffic to a website built 100% in Flash, which means the site cannot be found by search engines. Because the site cannot not be found / crawled by search engines it ends up losing a ton of traffic. It's great that you are online, but what's the point if no one knows!

It certainly isn't the search engines' fault; they just don't know that you exist.

Solution:

Depending on your website platform, you need to ask the hard questions about what is being done so that search engines can find your website and the different landing pages on your site. These elements can include, but are not exclusive to, your Title tags, descriptions, headings, W3C coding standards, proper URL naming conventions and automated XML sitemaps that submit new content to search engines. There are too many factors to name here, but I strongly suggest you do your own research and see what search engines think about your website.

There are a ton of free tools, like Google Webmaster, that can help you see what they see. Sign up today and get cracking.

Bad Stock Photography is Deathly

Good stock photography can help a website go from zero to hero. But if the photography is low quality, overused, or too corporate, your website visitors will be suffering from ad-blindness in seconds.

We've all seen it; the same blonde girl with a headset on and the call to action, *"We're here to help"*, next to it on the website. It's the conversion path less travelled, because it looks so fake that people assume the company is fake.

Your potential customers want to develop a relationship with your company, and pictures of fake people turn them off in seconds. They start questioning the legitimacy of your business or organization. *"Do they even exist?"; "Why don't they show real images of their staff"; "How can I trust a company that looks like a scam?"*

Solution:

Stop using the cheapest, most used images out there and find something that is original and high quality. Better yet, produce your own images! Don't like the way you look? Welcome to the club, you are not alone. Get over it and get snapping those photos.

CONTACT US!

WE'LL NEVER ANSWER...

If you are going to hire a photographer, take a look at their portfolio and ask yourself if you would put those pictures on your site. Make sure that they can work with your designer to get the shots necessary for the website (full body / headshots / team shots).

Oh, and make sure you are smiling.

#5

Your Website is Noisy

Did you know that the majority of web-surfing takes place during peoples' work day, between 9 and 5? People do their online banking at work, check Facebook, and they could be hitting your website during work hours too. They may even be hitting your site while sitting on the can.

There is a common assumption that a website that has sound equals a non-work related website. It may not be true that the person is slacking off, but we all know that everyone will judge the person when they hear a video come through their speakers.

If your website plays a video or makes any kind of sound, chances are your new visitor will shut your site down within 2 seconds. They will leave and they may never want to come back. You have just helped to expose and embarrass them and possibly incriminate them in slacking off in their workplace. Way to go.

Search Engines will wonder why no one stays on your website for more than 2 seconds and you will wonder why no one interacts with your site. You haven't given your website a chance to communicate anything.

I once had a customer that had their heart set on having a video of themselves walking onto the screen and giving a 3 minute sales-pitch to every website visitor that

hit their homepage. I was thankful that I talked them down to an embedded video that you had to click to play. I am sure that their customers were even more thankful.

Solution:

Give the controls over to your users. Embed videos, but **never have them auto-play,** no matter how much you want visitors to watch it. Avoid plugins or features on your site that use any kind of noise. Don't integrate walk-ons where visitors feel like someone has just invaded their screen and is trying to do a direct-sell. It's just offensive.

#6

Your Colour Scheme is Offensive

In the 80's, many fast food joints were accused of painting their interiors with 'irritating colours' to subconsciously influence their customers to want to leave the restaurant after they ate. The idea was, "Get them in, get their money, and get them out".

It should go without saying that your site should not follow that strategy. Unfortunately though, websites lose visitors simply because they use offensive colour schemes. If this is true of your site, then every page could be offending visitors subconscious thought, and as their heads start to hurt from the corporate yellows and bright greens being projected through their high-resolution screens, they will close your website down.

Some companies swear by their corporate colours, which may look great in print, but terrible when illuminated on a bright high-definition screen, 20 inches away from the customer's eyes. Don't try to give your prospects a suntan; they won't appreciate it.

Solution:

Venture away from colour combinations like blue & red, blue and yellow, green on red, or red on blue. Avoid using colours like yellow, bright green or red as the **majority** colour on your site.

If your branding colours are in these categories, create a different colour scheme for the web, or just knock out your logo's colour all together.

Make sure that you are using a consistent palate for the entire site. Use up to 6 colours and stick with them. No rainbow websites please.

Link-Building Killed Your Site

You read a convincing email from an international SEO Company that guarantees they can get your website to the top of search engines in as little as 6 weeks. You hire these "experts" and they set to work by placing links to your website on other 'Highly Ranked' sites that they guarantee will improve your PageRank™ value, and beat out the competition.

Little do you know, however, that the company that created PageRank™ (Google™) hates these kinds of practices. They have complex algorithms for searching and destroying these 'link farms' because they have no relevancy for users and are dishonest in their tactics.

These kinds of services can work for a few weeks, or maybe even a year. But as soon as Google™ discovers your link farm connections, your site is **penalized** and your ranking drops immediately[1]. You may even run the risk of never ranking again and worse still, your website is now effectively dead.

I personally get calls all of the time from prospective customers that have *all of a sudden* dropped from search engines, and they ask me how much it will cost to fix it. It is almost impossible to help websites that have ticked off

---

1 (Google n.d.)

search engines with unethical SEO methods because they are quick to judge and slow to trust.

Solution:

Do not buy false links from anyone.

Rather give users a reason to link to you. Consider writing a compelling blog filled with great information, build an online tool that people share with one another, or even publish some informative infographics or videos that help educate or entertain people. If you want people to link to you, you need to make it worth their while.

No Value = No Visitors.

People are coming to your site for a reason. They want to learn something, be educated, buy something, download resources, converse with you or perhaps be entertained. They are on a mission to get something from your website.

Imagine if you invited a bunch of friends over and didn't set out snacks, offer any drinks and had nothing to say to them. You certainly wouldn't be surprised if they left as quickly as they came and there would be no confusion as to the reason for them leaving. Companies tend to treat website visitors in the same way and yet are surprised when people leave their site. Visitors are simply voting with their feet. Your site offers them no reason to stay.

What are you doing to provide any value to the visitor? It may cost you money, time and resources to build a site worth visiting, but you need too! If you are selling a product that is a commodity in the market, why should they buy it from your site? What is your competitive advantage? What are you offering your visitors? If there is no value to visiting your site, they won't be around for long.

Solution:

Think about what you have to offer your visitors. If you don't have anything of value, think about resources you could create like blogs, videos, infographics, conversations, online tools, graphics or maybe an amazing product offering.

One of our customers, a technology company, increased their visitor to sales-lead conversion from 1% - 15% by offering a downloadable pricing PDF. A simple offer resulted in 15X the ROI on all of their online campaigns, overnight.

Remember that visitors are always thinking about WIIFM (what's in it for me), and they are looking to you to clearly provide the answer.

#9

Broken Links, Barren Site

Someone hits your website, clicks on a link and it doesn't go anywhere. Instead they see the frustrating *"404 – page not found"* error message. You may as well change the page to say, *'We don't spend any time on our site, and neither should you'*.

Your site is a barren wasteland of something that *used to be*. It's like entering an abandoned mall with signs that point to stores that went out of business years ago. Visitors assume it will only get worse the further into your site they go.

Broken links hurt your SEO (Search Engine Optimization), and most of all, they hurt your visitors' experience.

What is worse is when you don't know that your links are broken. Your customer will almost never tell you. Instead they will just leave quietly and go onto your competition's site, you know, the company with a working website!

Solution:

Hire a service that checks links on a regular basis. Find out about issues before your customer does, and reduce the risk of lost opportunity on minor things like links. We use a service called www.LinkTiger.com that can check a web-

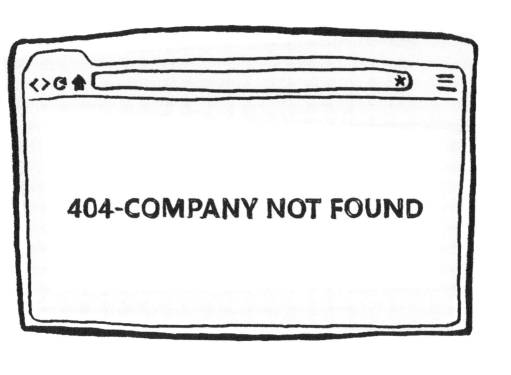

site for a few dollars per month and give you great reports that can be handed off to your web-designer or developer.

Alternatively, give someone in your office the task of checking the site on a regular basis and testing all of the features. They will hate their job, but you will save a few bucks…if they work for free.

Incomplete Sections ...Incompetent Company?

No website is ever complete. It is always a work in progress, but that does not give you license to *not finish* any pages that are accessible on the site.

It is simply embarrassing when a user hits a page on a website that is expected to be full of content and instead is greeted with a title saying 'Coming Soon!' This is pure stupidity. If you think that visitors are waiting with baited breath for your new ABOUT US page to hit the internet, think again.

Instead, visitors will leave with the impression that you just published a halfhearted project. You didn't manage your time wisely. You didn't have a project manager. You couldn't organize your company enough to write a few paragraphs about something. Whatever they think, it puts you in the doghouse.

Solution:

Don't tarnish your image with incompetence. Instead, drop the unfinished section from your website completely and make a plan to finish it. Consider whether you need this section at all. Unless you are a company that is unveiling a new project on a certain date, keep it off your site.

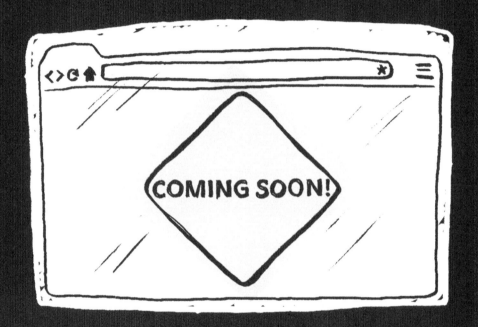

#11

No Pretty Buttons

Your website has a busy top navigation and pages and pages of paragraphs with links. Your drop down menus give people the impression they are doing research in an encyclopedia.

You decide to just use plain text hyperlinks at the end of paragraphs to help funnel people off to different sections of the site and you believe that they will read the entire paragraph to get there. After all, they want to spend 10-20 minutes on every page of your website…right? Wrong.

They do not want to read all your content to find out where to go. They want to click something!

Solution:

Give them buttons, and good ones too. Make the buttons interact when you put the curser over them so people know they work. Make the buttons obvious and put clear actionable words on them. Instead of saying 'Insurance Calculator', speak to their objectives and desires and say "Get a Quote".

Make sure your buttons stand out with a prominent colour or texture on the page. Don't hide them on the bottom of the page, or make them look like they were designed in the 90's. Make them shine!

Failure to Land

Driving all of your visitors to your homepage is like giving the same pitch to every customer, no matter what they are interested in.

Consider Apple.com. They have customers that come to their website looking to buy music, upgrade to the latest operating system, resolve an issue with their power supply, find a specific store's hours, or order 200 computers for a new school that is opening. Each of these visitors have different objectives, positions, and purchase habits.

That's why Apple.com doesn't try to say **everything that they do on one page.** Apple.com's homepage typically has the most recent product launch, or company announcement.

How do they manage to be growing in online sales? They funnel people into landing pages directly from search engines or campaigns. They speak directly into their target market's needs, wants and aspirations.

You may be thinking isn't that what navigation is for?

Well, yes, but only as a backup. Improving the user-experience has a direct correlation to improving conversion rates. If customers have to 'find' what they are looking for

through your navigation, or clicking on 2-3 links before getting what they want, they start to drop off. Customers that drop off are a waste of marketing dollars at work.

Solution:

Spend time defining your products, services and customers segments. Put each group into a different 'bucket' and even give them a name.

Example: If you sell T-shirts, you may have Sally, the Marketing Manager who is looking to buy T-shirts in bulk vs Gary, the teenager looking to buy a single shirt. List your customers and products and make sure you have a landing page strategy for each person that enters your website.

Build a marketing strategy behind **each page** with a targeted Call to Action that your target will respond too. Make it easy, and you'll get easy conversions.

#13

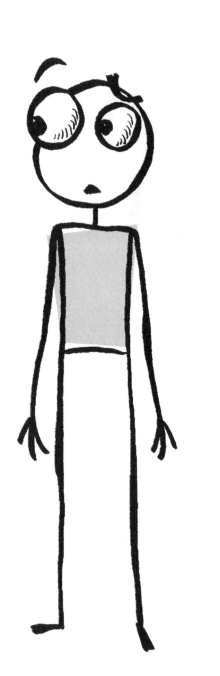

You're Playing Hide 'n Seek

Have you ever visited a site that doesn't list their pricing for common items? Or a retail store that doesn't tell you their hours of operation?

It is so frustrating.

A lot of businesses simply don't think about what customers are visiting their site for, or they purposely hide what the customer is after.

"If they find out our prices, they will just leave the site and never contact us." I hear this all too often. For some highly competitive businesses, this is not a demand that you can continue to ignore. If you are selling laptops or printers, you cannot expect everyone to call you to get a price.

Welcome to the internet my friend. If you can't compete with price on simple products, perhaps your business is actually failing? It's a hard fact, but in business we either stay competitive, or die a slow death. The internet has killed a lot of businesses that were never competitive in the first place.

If you are hiding something, most customers will assume that there is a reason why you are hiding it and they won't give you a second chance. They will just move on to the competition.

Solution:

For most businesses that are outside of the commodity market, you may have good reason to not list prices. You may not have set prices, or your quoting process may be too complex to have online. If this is your situation you should still **give people a simple, clear and directed way to get to what they need.**

Maybe it's a clear call to action with a few qualifying questions. Perhaps it's a *'Download Pricing'* call-to-action that will only be sent out once you have their email address. Provide multiple ways for them to get the information they are looking for, or assist them in connecting easily with someone that can help them. Give them a name, an email, a number or even a customer-focused form.

#14

Your Site Has GOTCHA's Behind Each Door

What if your website was successful in attracting visitors, engaging them in your content and converting them into a lead, sale or donor?

I'd say congratulations, but your job is not done. They have now entrusted you with their information, their money and / or purchase decision, but you tarnish their trust by sending them to a generic 'Thank You' page with no follow up content and no hint of what the next steps are.

That's like a guy asking for a girl's hand in marriage, and once he gets the ring on, gets up off his knee and goes to the fridge for a beer. Not very impressive. Within milliseconds of your customer trusting you with their decision, you drop them like a dirty shirt with nothing to do next. Deathly!

Customers going through this process feel cheated, or alienated. By the time you reach them, they feel disconnected from you and they may just not respond at all. Customers know when they are not being appreciated, and a generic *Thank you* page does just that.

Solution:

Think about what action your customer has just taken on your website. Consider carefully what content your customer immediately needs to receive to mitigate any buyer's remorse. Bring them to a page that walks them through the next step of being a lead, or customer. Give them confidence that they just made a great decision, and that you are still with them in the process.

In some cases, your site should send an automated email, but send it from a real email account that someone manages properly.

Dear Joe Customer,

I am Jessica, your account manager, and I just received your inquiry. I'll get back to you within the next hour about your request. You'll find attached our pricing guide for common products, if you are interested. Please call me directly if you have any questions in the meantime at 555-999-9999!

Sincerely, Jessica Awesome.

#15

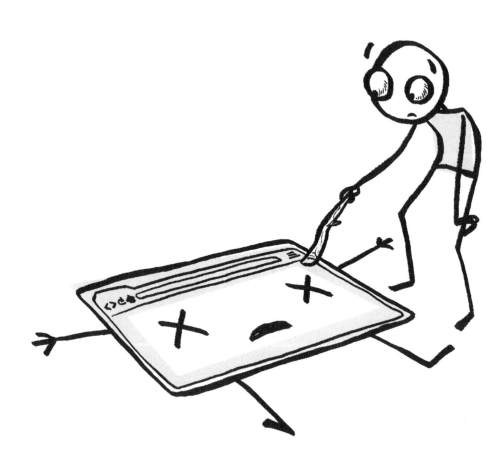

Connecting With a Corpse

It is scary how many companies count on a generic 'Contact us' page for lead-generation. There are two types of deaths when it comes to these useless forms.

First, the form may just be too generic and simple. Customers see the three fields (*Name / Email / Comments*) and get concerned that no one even monitors emails on this form. They fear that their email may get catapulted into cyberspace, never to find the person that their message was intended for. Maybe their email will get added to a marketing list that they didn't want to subscribe too. They quickly leave the page because their fears about relevancy outweigh their need to connect with the company.

The second death is the exact opposite. You try to get the customer to choose a hundred different options to find the right department. You ask them required questions they don't know the answers too. The form is longer than the terms & conditions on a cell phone contract and not one of the fields automatically get filled by their browser's memory. They see your form as more of a litmus test than a way of contacting someone. They leave your site, annoyed by your attempt to capture too much, too soon.

Solution:

Don't depend on one form for everything. Instead have multiple forms on the site that are geared towards your visitors need. Don't pack it with required fields, but allow them to decide what to submit. Start with asking questions that they care about like, "*What are you interested in?*" instead of gathering information that you care about like *Name / email / phone*. Make the form easy to fill out, attractive to the eye and give them helpful hints as they go through it.

If the form **needs** to be long, break it up into multiple steps so they don't get overwhelmed by scrolling before committing to your form. After you launch the form, test it with real people and see what they think. You'll be surprised how many people drop off because of one single question.

One of our clients sold boat insurance and had a 1% visitor to lead conversion ratio in their quoting engine. The form was long, daunting and full of technical speak. We redesigned the site to have '3 easy steps' and the conversion ratio skyrocketed to 65% overnight. It wasn't rocket science; we just made the process simple for the user.

#16

Navigation Overkill

Someone hits your site looking for information. Their eyes are greeted with 14 top headings in your navigation, which all have dropdowns. Once they go onto another page, they now have two or three different tiers of navigation and their eyes start to cross. Every page has become a new adventure, running through doors like Alice in Wonderland, with no way to get back home.

You decide that every section of your site requires a new page, so if someone wants to read about your company, they have to visit 7 different pages.

Bewildered, they keep going through the site and realize that they are now on another website, but with a similar top navigation. They just want to go home and start again. Tears follow. You get the point.

Solution:

Throw your current site in the trash. Stop trying to tinker with something that has become horrendously overgrown over the years and start thinking about your users and how they want to relate with your business.

Build a sitemap on a blank piece of paper and start combining areas in similar buckets that makes sense to

your customers. Most businesses or organizations may have difficulty whittling this list down, because every department / section may believe they deserve their own heading on the homepage. Work it down to 6 or less headings, and think about the other areas that can move around the page. Less important pages (about us / careers / contact / locations) can move into your footer, depending on your business.

Instead of creating a page for each topic, consider putting more information on one page, and having different 'sections' that a user can scroll through. Scrolling through information is very acceptable to online visitors, as long as it's presented neatly and accompanied with a nice design. Go ahead and make your new sitemap! There's no time to waste!

I once met with a client that told me their business was too complex for a simple navigation, and needed 17 top headings for their users. In the end, we were able to rationalize the navigation down to only 6 items, and their users found the new site easier to use.

Your Site Uses Images Instead of Text

To the naked eye, you won't be able to spot this on your website, but it is a silent killer! Some web-designers cut corners in their work by creating an image of text, rather than have the text in the HTML. This method could be used anywhere on your site and it can cause serious user issues.

First, search engines cannot read text that is imbedded within images. Yes, that's correct, they cannot read it! This means that they cannot index this content for users and include it in search results. If your main headings or calls to action are all images, this doesn't mean anything to crawlers.

Second, users cannot highlight or copy this content. This may not seem like a big deal, but consider someone trying to copy your information into an email they are sending, or your address into their address book. Consider mobile phones that are now integrated to treat 7 or 10 consecutive numbers as phone numbers that can be clicked. Potential customers are not able to simply click on your number to call and they will leave, unimpressed and frustrated.

Solution:

When you are building your site, specify to your web-designer and developers that you need all of your text content to be in the HTML code. Forbid any text areas being made into an image, unless approved by you and with good reasons.

To test out your website, try and copy + paste content from your website into a word document. If you can't copy it, it's just an image. Get it fixed.

#18

Coming on Too Strong

Yes, you are trying to convert people on your website. I get it. They get it. But if you come on too strong, they may be frightened by your approach and leave the site.

Like a bad date, you repel people with your cheap gimmicks, hard-sales tactics and flashing offers. DON'T CREATE ANNOYING CONTENT THAT SCREAMS AT EVERY VISITOR. These sites do not build confidence. They scare people away from ever dealing with you.

There may be a few misguided individuals that fall for your animated gif's, crappy sales videos and extra, EXTRA large call-to-action buttons, but most will run screaming for the hills.

Solution:

If you are trying to impress visitors, show off your awesomeness without selling yourself cheap. Impress them by being confident in your offering and giving them the keys to respond.

Your visitors are not stupid and they won't click on every button you throw at them. Give them calls-to-action that are not evasive or desperate. If you find that your site isn't convincing, consider changing your calls-to-action instead of just making it bigger.

#19

Your Site is Not Mobile Responsive

Users hate mobile sites. They may look *okay* in their browser, but users feel cheated if you don't provide them with the information they need. Mobile sites are typically a scaled down version of a company's information, including their contact details, a few product sections and maybe a map.

The stats are in and showing that users are abandoning these mobile sites in droves to visit the real website, even if it doesn't look great in a mobile / tablet browser[2]. They don't want to miss out on your real content because typically mobile sites don't have what they are looking for.

Solution:

Whoever is building your site should make your entire website **mobile responsive**. Responsive websites work on every platform (desktop / tablet / mobile) and on every operating system. It doesn't just *look like your website,* **it IS your website!**

Responsive sites are built with a foundation to expand / shrink based on the browser size and collapse content based on the user. They enable you to make every page 'mobile compatible' without having to build another mobile-only site.

---

2 (Miller 2012)

Save money, time and your customer's patience by switching to a **mobile responsive design.**

Yawn...Too Many Pages

You want to do research on a company and venture over to their 'about us' section. You are now presented with a sub-navigation of links all pointing to different pages. 'Our History, Our Future, Mission, Vision, Values, Executive Team, Board of Directors, Past Members, Location, Philosophy, Community Involvement...blah blah blah' and the list goes on. Each of these sections contain a paragraph of text that will never be read, and will likely be updated every 10 years.

I am not saying that these *sections* are not important, but do you really expect your customer to go through each link on your navigation and read each paragraph? Do you think they want to go on a wild goose chase to get the information they need? Do you think it's a fun experience for anyone who is quickly reviewing your company, on their phone, while sitting in a coffee shop? Your website just killed them with boredom.

Solution:

Think about your customer and what they want to see. Then review all content through that filter and cut out anything that customers don't care about.

Take sections that are similar and make plans to combine them into one page with multiple areas. If you are working with a good web-designer, they will be able to make some suggestions. Poor designers will simply pack all of the content onto one page, without any design thought.

If you are not getting what you need out of your web-designer, consider switching! You can't force someone to be creative with content. Find a seasoned designer and allow them to help you get this right.

Socially Dead

When someone hits your site, you want them to speak with you. Besides online chat software, Social Media is a direct connection that they can use to communicate back and forth with you. But most company's social media strategy is simply including links to your social properties. Do this and your web presence is as good as dead.

So your company is on YouTube, but what does that even mean? Are you producing good content? Is YouTube going to help them answer the question that they have about your product? It may, but your customers don't know that.

Even worse is when websites have a crazy list of Social Media properties that they don't use. It's like having a 1-800 that nobody answers. It would be better to do nothing at all.

Solution:

Consider which Social Media networks you can commit to being active on. You can't do all of them well, so choose the ones that your customers are on and **have a presence there.**

Instead of integrating icons, **integrate their feeds.** Don't just tell people to *Join us on Facebook,* but show what your Facebook community is talking about with a live feed! All of a sudden, your stale website will be regularly updated with real content that you are publishing on a regular basis.

Your website now has a heartbeat and a voice. You are well on your way to having a web-presence instead of just another "dead" web-site.

#22

Your Website is Faceless

I believe that, without question, any successful living website needs a blog. Many businesses have blogs, but don't have any stated authors. *Someone* is writing this content, but who? Why should I trust them? If I like the article, who do I give credit too? If I comment, who is going to answer?

Faceless websites are difficult to connect to, for obvious reasons. It is not normal for people to build relationships with corporations and generic articles with no personality. Brands all over the world are changing, using peoples face on Social Media instead of logos. Think about how people became Apple™ lovers because of Steve Jobs, to an almost cultish extent, or consider how Mashable™ **is** Peter Cashmore.

If you have a faceless company, it will be difficult to engage with people online on a real level.

Solution:

If you have a blog, list the author and connect it with Google Plus Authorship program[3]. Get a picture of them next to their article, so you can see the person who is speaking. If you have a Twitter account, consider promot-

3   (Google n.d.)

ing the person who mans the account every day. If you have multiple users / authors, allow them to sign off on every communication.

I would rather ask for help from 'Sally from WestJet' than some generic social media centre for inquiries.

Stop creating static sites and start building relationships with real people.

#23

You are Speaking AT Your Customers

Poor, ineffective website content is written from an 'us and them' perspective. Visitors are talked at, instead of being engaged with content that encourages a conversation and speaks to their thoughts, aspirations, emotions and needs. Visitors are treated as targets with a huge bull's eye on their wallets.

Never asking for feedback, or ignoring customer comments is a sure way to alienate your potential customers. Go ahead and close off the comments on the blog, don't respond on Social Media and don't ask anyone to create any content. That's the best way to tell your customers that not only are they **not 'a part' of your business**, but they are a nuisance to deal with as well.

Solution:

Use language that is inclusive of website visitors. Drop the corporate speak and talk to them, and with them, about what you do. Use real language and don't worry about putting everything into a full sentence. For your Calls-To-Action, use language that is actionable, and attractive for people to click. Instead of '*Register for the Feb 21st, 2015 event*', what about '*Reserve my seat!*'

Allow them to interact with content with *comments* and *likes*, and enable them to submit their own content if you can. Amazon.com™ is North America's #1 online retailer and one of the main reasons why people come to the site is because of the User Reviews, not just their "1 Click Shipping" options[4].

If you want to breathe life back into your website, stop the monologue and start conversing.

---

4   (Thau 2014)

#24

No traffic plan

You launch a beautiful site that engages and converts every user that comes across it, but no one visits it. Your site just joined the 900 million websites[5] online today and is already dead in the water. A car without gas, a cell phone without a battery, a store without a storefront, a light bulb without a socket. You get the picture.

I once had a customer ask me what Google's phone number was and after asking why they needed it, they told me that they needed to tell Google that their site went live and to put them 'on the top'. Scary stuff. Without traffic, your site is dead. Without visitors, there are no customers. Without a quantifiable traffic plan, you are an aimless ship, drifting in the dark.

Solutions:

There are tons of ways to generate traffic, but you need to start with a plan to get the right kind of traffic. Who do you want to visit your site? Moms in Southern California? CEO's in New York? People searching for 17" monitors that are waterproof?

Once you know your target audience, consider how you can show up across their screens. Search Engine Mar-

---

5   (Bowes 2014)

keting (SEM) is ideal for businesses that people are already looking for. Social Marketing is ideal for building relationships with your targets and current customers. Whatever your avenue is, make a plan for the type of traffic that your website needs to be considered successful.

#25

You Lack Testimonials

Your website clearly states how awesome you really are. Of course you are; it's your website and you wrote the content. You boast about your sales, service, offering, competitive advantage and mission statement. It may help the customer understand what you think about yourself, but what about other customers?

Do your customers think the same things? I am not talking about text base, generic statements that you have on your website like "I love how I am treated by ABC Company; they offer great prices for schools! – John D." Do you trust that generic, nameless, faceless recommendation? Neither do your customers. Testimonials are rated as one of the best pieces of content you can have on your website, and yet most companies don't think about how to produce this effectively[6].

Solution:

Give customers ways to submit their feedback to your company on a regular basis. You'll never get what you don't ask for. Ask them to spend a few minutes and give honest, candid feedback about your business. The results may surprise you, hopefully in a good way.

6   (Dean 2014)

OUTSTANDING

I LOVED HOW I WAS TREATED HERE

THANKS!

GREAT SERVICE

AMAZING!

When posting testimonials online, work on getting good images of these people to give a face behind a name, and even a city. Want to really impress people? Launch video testimonials and allow your customers to speak in front of a camera. There are businesses that are built around video testimonials that do an outstanding job of pulling the gold out of people like www.SeeMyClients.com.

Let your customers speak for you.

You Aren't Offering Visitors Candy

You want your visitors to **do something** on your site, but you don't offer them any incentives. You want them to fill out forms, but all they get is their name on a list that will be actively marketed too.

They don't care about you. They don't want to just be a sale or a lead. They know they have value, and they don't come cheap. Remember that online users are constantly asking themselves WIIFM (what's in it for me)? It's time to answer them.

Marketing online without incentives is like inviting someone into your office sales meeting and not providing the coffee and snacks. It's just rude.

Solution:

Give them candy. By candy, I mean anything that will be pleasing for them, or benefit them in some way. Offer them a chance to win something, even the product they are interested in. Give them a downloadable product that is worth something, an e-book, a PDF, a whitepaper. Something!

Even if you are dealing with businesses, these businesses have **real people** that are visiting your website that eat,

drink and live their own lives. I am not saying to cheapen your brand with crappy consumer goods, but consider products that the majority of the public would be happy to have. Give away an iPad, an Amazon gift card, a month of free service. Do whatever it takes to add that extra **push** for users to take action.

Still Using Flash...Seriously?

Honestly, where have you been the past five years? Flash is dead. The final nail in the coffin was Steve Job's letter to Adobe in 2010[7].

Get rid of it right away. Even flash banners or custom forms need to go because of the issues that they are causing.

Google hates flash because they cannot index the content in it, and they can't send users to the right page. Apple doesn't support flash on any of their mobile / tablet devices. Customers hate flash because it takes too long to load. Marketers hate flash because it isn't as flexible as standard HTML / CSS sites.

Using Flash is digital suicide.

Solutions:

Most companies used flash because it improved graphics or interaction with users. Interactive interfaces, moving components, and nifty features that just *looked good*. A lot of these objectives can now be accomplished with different browser technologies like JavaScript and jQuery. It may take more web development skills to build these features into your site, but it will improve your website interaction.

---

7   (Apple 2010)

Content Killers

You launched your website; good job! You integrated a blog because you recognized that you need to get active in content marketing; great work. You haven't updated your blog in 18 months and you've asked your web-designer to remove the dates on all articles. Total failure.

Your web-presence should talk to your customers. It should be a place where they see what you are up to, your innovations, and your company advancements. Blogs are central to communicating online, and dormant blogs communicate just that – you're dead.

A dead blog = a dead website. It lets everyone know that you are good at planning out what you want to sell people on your website, but not great on the follow through and execution. Today's business does not have any excuse for not blogging.

Solutions:

Create a plan **and** assign someone to own it. Blogs that are left to company owners or sales people are generally left in the dust as soon as the person assigned gets busy doing their job. I am not saying that Presidents shouldn't blog, because they really should, but they shouldn't be the one responsible for keeping on top of it.

Create a blog schedule with topics each month / quarter / year and authors that will be contributing to it. Don't think the blog will fill itself when you have a spare moment; it will never happen.

#29

Your Website Only Works for 50% of Users

Have you ever visited a site that looks terrible or broken? Most of the time it's because of the version of your browser. Although operating systems are getting better at performing automatic updates, there are still a lot of users on outdated technologies (IE7) that just don't seem to get it.

It doesn't matter why the website is broken, typically the user on an outdated browser won't know how to fix it. They just leave.

I once worked with an insurance company that had a quoting tool that didn't work on Google Chrome. This represented over 50% of their website traffic that left frustrated and with a poor image of the brand. In the years they spent money on quality traffic, they had never tried the site themselves and the end result was depressing; a low conversion ratio and lack of new business.

Solution:

Be your customer. Test it yourself. It may take a while to test your entire site with every browser, but it's great insurance against a broken experience. Test it on your phone, tablet, desktop, and a friend's computer. You might even want to ask your friends or family to complete a few actions on it. Try your forms, videos, shopping carts, everything.

Consider using programs like www.BrowserStack.com that can test multiple browsers simultaneously, and give you results that you can take back to your developers. Be ruthless in testing.

Your Content Management System Died Years Ago

There are some content management systems (CMS) that are dead by design. Built years ago, and without the capability to grow and change with the rest of the web, they have nothing left to offer. These platforms may have worked well at one time, but the new web is a social web and if your platform could not migrate, it's as good as dead.

What does this look like? Watch out for things like strange URL structures. If your URL's look like www.website.com/=p?2938?noresults instead of www.website.com/shop/camera/, you have a problem.

Well-meaning design companies still use some of these platforms because they have not updated themselves from using old programs and have more experience launching these old kinds of sites. They are typically not mobile compatible, nor are they search engine friendly or easy to administer.

Solution:

Time for a fresh start. Select a platform that has signif-
icant market share and is used by lots of companies. That
way you aren't looking to replace it any time soon. Nothing
lasts forever, but I personally think it should at least last
you 8-10 years.

My company uses open source programs like Word-
Press to power all of our web-presences, and we have
benefited from years of updates and improvements that the
development community has added. They are easy to use,
update and integrate with other programs. Jump on the
CMS bandwagon and enjoy the benefits of open-source
programming.

It's also free, and that's just good news.

#31

Not Enough Roads Leading To Rome

You may have a certain way you like to communicate. You probably have certain routes that you like to travel to work. But there are more ways to communicate and travel than just the ones you happen to like.

If you are a part of the Millennial generation, texting and social media are your preferred methods of communication, and phone calls scare you. Phone calls are considered a full frontal social attack for this generation, and choosing to make a call is like choosing to get a root canal.

On the other hand, Boomers love making phone calls and their days are consumed with writing and responding to emails. They have no problem calling a company to get something.

If your website doesn't have multiple roads to your final destination, you are making it difficult for people to relate with you. Don't like to connect with people on social media? If your customers do, then you'll have to adapt. After all, it is all about the way **they** want to communicate, not you.

Solution:

Consider different types of people that are on your website and find out **their preferred method of contact.** Better yet, offer many options and see which route they take.

These days you need to offer more than a few methods. Electronic communication has taken many different forms that you need to consider. Phone, email, forms, live chat, text, Twitter, Facebook Pages and LinkedIn are all mediums that you should evaluate for your business.

#32

You Are S-L-O-W.

You website is amazing. Too bad it takes 12 seconds to load your homepage. The internet keeps speeding up, it's difficult to find a place without WIFI these days, but everything slows to a deathly crawl when reaching your site.

Why? Great question, and it's one you should have for your web designer / developer and even hosting company. There are tons of factors when it comes to website speed, and one bottle neck in the system will slow everything down.

Even search engines penalize sites for slow site performance because they don't want to send their precious searches to a site that is encountering delays. A few small seconds is a big deal online.

Solution:

Ask the hard questions and test it for yourself. There are a ton of online tools that will run through your site and give it a speed rating in comparison with other websites. Google even provides a ton of free tools to help you troubleshoot the issues yourself in Google Webmasters™ so that you can visually see how your site performs[8].

_____

8   (Google 2013)

You may need to bring the results to your web developer or hosting company to resolve, but it will give you a good indication of where the problems are coming from.

#33

You're Using Corporate Speak

People aren't impressed with corporate speak. It is alienating and creates a disconnect between you and your customers. There are better ways to impress. You've been on sites where the content looks like a bunch of business words jammed together in 10-point font. It's awful. You know what I mean...

"If you objectively benchmark all client-centric processes, your implementation process through web-enabled capital will generate exponential ROI."

Exactly.

Why do you do this? Maybe it's because you are trying to impress your customers. Or you don't know how to simplify your messaging. If you are unable to communicate your value proposition in plain English, your website is pulseless and in need of a content defibrillator.

Solution:

Stop using words that belong in a Macro-economic textbook and start using words that you would use to describe your business to a 12 year old. Better yet, hire someone to write your content and only spend an hour to

two explaining what you do with a whiteboard. Get some fresh eyes on the project and you may just find that content that converses is content that converts!

Review every area of your website and think about your users' entire experience. Think about thank you pages, 404 page messages and even your error messages. Instead of your form errors telling the user to, "*Please correct the following errors*", encourage them to try again, saying, "Oops, did you make a mistake entering your email address?"

#34

No Videos...What?

You have seconds, or at most a minute, to communicate your offering to new users who **don't like to read.** At best, they skim through content, just like you're skimming through this book, stopping every once in a while when you find something interesting.

If a picture says a thousand words, then video says a million. People love watching videos to learn about products, services, trends and news. There are 4 BILLION YouTube views a day[9]. Yes, that's Billion with a B. Stats show that landing pages with embedded video can get up to 80% more conversions[10].

Solution:

Choose areas of your website that you believe would be enhanced with video. Your homepage and main product landing pages are all prime targets for video. Think about what your customer needs to see, or have explained and choose a style that would suit your site.

At Candybox, we have used sites like *live Fiverr.com* to produce short videos for $5 to help our visitors understand what we are trying to communicate. You don't need to break the bank to get into video, but you do need to have a plan.

9   (YouTube 2012)
10 (Eyeview n.d.)

#35

Your Site is Ugly, Really Ugly.

So you got a good deal on your website, because your brother knew a guy that worked with someone internationally that could put up your website for $500. Yeah, it looks like it. You get what you pay for.

Unfortunately for most companies, they suffer from what I call 'Web-Child Blindness'. Since they love the content they wrote, and are so excited to see anything about their company online, they love their ugly website at first sight. Their new baby has come into the world and they are proud to show it off to all of their friends. No one tells them that it's ugly, they don't ask for honest feedback, and they think their website is gorgeous. The main problem is that this website shouldn't be designed for you; it's for your customer.

Your website is ugly, and your customer, whether you like it or not, assumes that an unprofessional website **equals** an unprofessional company.

I don't care how much money you *saved,* you just **lost** a bunch of potential customers.

Solution:

Start off by caring about your customer, and their opinions. Set aside a nice budget for the new site, depending on the size of your company and make time to understand the importance of creating a site that looks nice.

Next, build a 'wish list' of what you want the website to **DO.** It's not just about pretty pictures, but a pretty design on a functional website that has a purpose. You should submit this list, either in an RFP / RFI to web companies that have *impressive portfolios, not just a good sales pitch.*

Review a number of portfolios and ask the hard questions. What was the goal of their website projects (besides just being pretty) and did it meet / exceed these goals? Contact these companies' customers and find out if they enjoyed the experience of launching their project and if it exceeded their expectations.

Make sure you select a vendor that agrees with your requirements, and has demonstrated measurable results.

Too Much Content

Stop writing content that will never be read by anyone. People read online, but only in chunks. The more you write, the greater the chance that no one will ever read your droning's about your topic.

SEO companies may recommend writing thousands of words on a page to improve Search Engine value, but a lot of this is based in fiction. Search Engines love content that engages people.

There are algorithms that Search Engines use to determine whether users are finding value on your website and reading the content. Time on site, bounce rate, and engaged users (clicks) are all metrics that are feeding the beast and helping programs determine if people are engaging on your page.

Solution:

If you want to write a lot, consider saving it for a blog, downloadable PDF, or even an e-Book. Don't give away the farm on your homepage and expect new visitors to trust you are worth the read. Content is king, but you need to organize yourself or else it will be overwhelming for your readers.

How much should you write? There is no simple answer, but write enough to get your point across effectively.

Your Business is Broken.

No one responds to your website offers and it doesn't matter how convincing your website is, or the budget that you've put into advertising, or the time you've spent on driving traffic. If this is your scenario you may have to face facts; some businesses just don't work online.

I've turned down projects that I didn't believe would succeed online. There is no point in flogging a dead horse with tons of advertising dollars. Some businesses don't work for a variety of reasons including poor pricing, stupid products, or external sources like competition, environmental issues and the list goes on.

Some people think that you can do *anything* on the web, and they can always find *some sucker* to buy it. It's just not true. Online users are more educated than ever before and they know a bad product when they see one.

Solution:

Don't waste your time. Fix the business model before you launch it. If you can, find offline customers that validate your product before you throw away thousands online. There are some businesses that just don't work, plain and simple.

CONCLUSION:

WHAT NOW?

So, if your worst fears have been confirmed and you realize that your website is effectively dead; you are now like most other businesses! Most companies I meet with are identifying the same things you are and they are choosing to move away from traditional website formats and embrace an interactive, conversion focused web-presence. Like it or not, your website represents who your company is. Poor quality sites portray poor quality companies. Not fair? I agree, but it's a fact of life in a digital world.

So what are you going to do about it?

You can have a dynamic web-presence that drives sales and improves your customer experience, but it takes work. There are no shortcuts online. You have to deliberately plan and strategize your end game before you get your designers and developers involved. They should be brought in near the middle of the project, and not the beginning. It is great to get their input, but they cannot be the ones running the show anymore.

Stop staring at your old website. Take a clean break from what you have done, and try building it to reflect where you want to go. Pick a direction that you will be happy with in five years' time because, as your company grows, it's unlikely you'll have the time to reinvent your presence every few years.

There are more ditches than freeways online. As a business, you need to be aware of what doesn't work and get rid of the clutter as fast as you can. Every website project I have ever worked on has started off with the same direction from the client, "*We want it to be simple*". That's the hope and dream of every new web-presence, and you need to fight to protect it, every step of the way.

Don't build it by committee, vote, or with people that haven't built a web-presence that converts users online. They may know what they like, but that doesn't mean they can lead the design direction. I love art, but I wasn't able to draw the simple stick figures in this book.

Every day, your competitors are reinventing the way they attract, engage and convert users into advocates. There is a fight for online market share and you'd be smart to get in before your industry gets too crowded.

Hopefully by this point, you have learned how to avoid most website perils. Now it's time to create something living and watch it grow into a raging success.

Enjoy the journey.

Works Cited

Apple. *Thoughts on Flash.* 2010. http://www.apple.com/ hotnews/thoughts-on-flash/ (accessed May 27, 2014).

Bowes, Matt. *How Many Websites Are There in January 2014?* January 18, 2014. http://www.techmadee-asy.co.uk/2014/01/18/many-websites-january-2014/ (accessed May 27, 2014).

Dean, Marie. *How & Why You Should Invest In Getting Good Testimonials w/ Examples.* January 29, 2014. http:// conversionxl.com/how-why-you-should-invest-in-getting-good-testimonials-w-examples/#. (accessed May 27, 2014).

Eyeview. "Making Video Accountable." http://www. eyeviewdigital.com/documents/EyeView-White-Pa-per-Making-Video-Accountable.pdf (accessed May 22, 2014).

Google. *Google Authorship.* https://plus.google.com/authorship (accessed 2014).

— *Link Schemes- Webmaster.* https://support.google.com/webmasters/answer/66356?hl=en (accessed 2014).

— *PageSpeed Tools.* July 9, 2013. https://developers.google.com/speed/page speed/insights/ (accessed May 27, 2014).

Miller, Miranda. *72% of Consumers Want Mobile-Friendly Sites: Google Research.* September 26, 2012. http://searchenginewatch.com/article/2208496/72-of-Consumers-Want-Mobile-Friendly-Sites-Google-Research (accessed May 27, 2014).

Thau, Barbara. "Interbrand Reveals The 'Best Retail Brands' Of 2014 (And The Biggest Losers)." *Forbes.* April 8, 2014. http://www.forbes.com/sites/barbarathau/2014/04/08/interbrand-reveals-the-best-retail-brands-of-2014-and-the-biggest-losers/ (accessed May 27, 2014).

YouTube. *Official Blog.* January 23, 2012. http://youtube-global.blogspot.ca/2012/01/holy-nyans-60-hours-per-minute-and-4.html (accessed May 22, 2014).

About the Author

Darrell Keezer founded Candybox Marketing, a digital marketing agency, in 2008, at the age of 23 and quickly became a recognized leader in Digital Marketing Campaigns, with a broad and influential client base in Canada and the USA.

Darrell is a leading Digital Marketing expert, assisting clients across multiple industries to make the switch from traditional advertising and reducing their marketing carbon footprint. He is a sought after speaker and has given keynote addresses at many Marketing and Entrepreneurship events across the country, inspiring companies to embrace how their customers have changed.

With a passion for equipping the next generation of marketers, Darrell has built a young, effective team who are pushing the limits of where traditional agencies have gone. As a graduate of Sheridan College (Business Administration Marketing, 2005), Darrell has enjoyed numerous opportunities to interact with and influence the Sheridan student body, assisting with the direction of the Marketing program and hiring Sheridan Graduates. Darrell was inducted into the Sheridan Faculty of Business Hall of Fame in 2014.

Married with four children, Darrell believes strongly in giving back and he prioritizes serving several *Not for Profits* each year, assisting them to market themselves online and to effectively engage with their donors.

You can connect with him on most social networks by visiting www.about.me/darrellkeezer

Candybox: Our Sweet Story

Candybox Marketing is a Digital Marketing Agency focused on generating new customers online. Through web design, social media services and search marketing strategies, we help companies build an online presence that attracts, engages and converts people into customers. Candybox Marketing has become a preferred supplier of online marketing services across multiple industries since its launch in 2008.

Built with a goal to make the web sweet, Candybox has enjoyed unprecedented success and is a recognized leader in Digital Marketing Campaigns, serving a broad and influential client base across the USA and Canada. With clients including FOX Broadcasting, Spin Master Toys, IBAO, KwikKopy and the Toronto Police Department, Candybox has launched hundreds of lead generation and creative social media campaigns that have been used as case studies in many industry publications.

With a focus on implementing new initiatives that better support clients' success, our Social Media Workshops have seen over 1000 businesses trained in the benefits of integrating social media and building customer relationships online.

Our company has enjoyed continual growth and expansion as the need for Digital Marketing has grown dramatically in the past decade.

The message is clear: If your business is not committed to digital marketing and connecting with your customers online, it's time to rethink how you do business.

CPSIA information can be obtained at www.ICGtesting.com
Printed in the USA
LVOW05s0411131114

413166LV00006B/35/P